A Child's First Book of
Bible Stories

by Wanda Hayes

Illustrations by
Kathryn Hutton/Heidi Petach

STANDARD PUBLISHING
Cincinnati, Ohio
2949

Library of Congress Cataloging in Publication Data

Hayes, Wanda.
   A child's first book of Bible stories.

   Summary: Forty-seven Old and New Testament stories,
from the Creation to John's view of the Heavenly City.
   1. Bible stories, English. [1. Bible stories]
I. Hutton, Kathryn, ill. II. Petach, Heidi, ill.
III. Title.
BS551.2.H39 1983   220.9'505   83-664
ISBN 0-87239-659-2

Introduction

A Child's First Book of Bible Stories is especially for the very young child who has not yet learned to read. It contains stories from both the Old and New Testaments to be read aloud to the child. The stories start with the creation in Genesis and end with John's view of Heaven in Revelation.

This is a special book for special people. You will notice that the word "special" is used as the theme idea for the various sections.

The stories are special, too. They were carefully chosen to give young children an overview of the entire Bible while they are at the impressionable preschool age.

Most children love to have stories read to them. This book will provide the parent, grandparent, or teacher with a source of reading joy for any small child.

A Child's First Book of Bible Stories can be read at bedtime, used for family devotions with small children, or read anytime for fun. Be sure to talk about the stories with the child and explain anything he or she might not understand about the times in which the stories took place and unfamiliar Bible words.

The illustrations were drawn by two different artists. One did the Old Testament and the other the New Testament. This gives variety and enrichment to the stories, and helps the child to learn even more about the Bible.

We have tried to make the art as well as the stories as Biblically accurate as possible. Our hope and prayer is that *A Child's First Book of Bible Stories* will introduce children to the Bible and lead them to love God's Word.

Contents

God Made Everything SPECIAL

God's SPECIAL Helpers

God's SPECIAL People

God's SPECIAL Son

Jesus' SPECIAL Work

Jesus' SPECIAL Friends Do His SPECIAL Work

Heaven: Our SPECIAL Home

God Made Everything Special

8

God's Beautiful World

At the very start of our world, there was no light at all. It was very dark. Then God's Spirit moved over the dark, wet earth, and He said, "Let light start to shine." And it did because when God tells something to happen, it happens.

God said, "The light is good." Then He divided the light from the darkness. God also said, "I will call the light 'day' and the darkness 'night.' " And that evening, and that morning were the very first day.

On the second day of the world, God made the sky above the wet, shapeless earth.

On the third day, God said, "Let all of the water on the earth come together so I can see dry land." And that is what happened. God watched the waters run together and called them seas.

When the water ran together into seas, it left big, big patches of dry land—hills, valleys, mountains, rocks, and sand. God looked at them and said, "I will call the dry land earth." Then He said, "The earth and the seas that I have made are good."

God looked again at the dry land and said, "I will make all kinds of plants and fruit trees to grow on the earth. And I will put seeds in them so there will be more and more plants and trees on the earth I have made." Then all kinds of plants and fruit trees began to grow just as God told them to. And there was evening and morning—one more day.

On the fourth day, God looked at the sky above His earth and said, "I need big lights to shine on my earth to rule the day and the night." So He made the big, bright sun and put it in the sky to shine on the earth in the daytime. And He made the big, round moon and put it in the sky to shine on the earth in the nighttime. Then God filled the wide heavens with millions of bright, shiny stars. When He was through, God looked at the sun, the moon, and the millions of stars He had made and placed in the sky. God said, "They are all very good."

On the fifth day, God filled the seas and rivers with every kind of fish and sea creature that could live in them. He made them so there would be more and more— the whales would make more whales, the frogs would make more frogs, and the fish would make more fish.

After God made all kinds of fish, He filled the skies with beautiful and interesting birds. He made some that fly in the sky and some that just walk around on the earth. He made birds with different shapes like ducks and swans. He made them with feathers every color of the rainbow. The earth and sky were even more beautiful with all of the pretty birds.

God must have been very happy and excited about His new creations. The seas and skies were full of them. But He was not finished. On the sixth day, God made animals to live on His earth. He made cows and pigs and wild animals like tigers and lions. He made small animals like squirrels and tall ones like giraffes. And He made sure there would be more and more animals to fill His beautiful earth. God looked at His creatures and said, "They are good. I like them all."

In six days, God made a beautiful world and filled it with all kinds of plants and animals, but He was not finished yet. Before the sun went down on the sixth day, God said, "Now, I will make the most important creation of all."

The First People

On the sixth day, God also made His last and best creation. God took some of the dirt from the ground and made a man. God breathed into him, and the man became alive. Then God made a beautiful garden for the man in a place called Eden. He put the man He had made in the garden and named him Adam.

Adam saw a beautiful sight when he looked at the garden. He saw all kinds of delicious fruit hanging from the trees.

God told Adam, "You may eat as much of the fruit from these trees as you want. But there is one tree in the garden that you must not touch. You cannot eat the fruit of that one tree."

Adam had lots of work to do every day. He took care of the trees in the garden. He named all of the animals and fish that God had made. But God said, "Adam should not be the only person here in the garden. He needs someone to be here with him."

Then God did a very wonderful thing. He made Adam go to sleep, and while he was sleeping, God took one of his ribs. Then He closed the place on Adam's body where He had removed it. And while Adam was still asleep, God took the rib and made a woman to be Adam's helper. God brought the woman to Adam, and she became his helper. Adam named her Eve. He liked her very much, and they lived together in the Garden of Eden. They were the very first people in the world. God had made the beautiful world for them—His best creation.

Adam and Eve
Leave the Garden

Adam and Eve were very happy in the beautiful garden that God had made for them. They loved to take care of the trees. They enjoyed watching the animals walking through the garden. They enjoyed hearing the songs of the birds and seeing the fish swim in the rivers. They liked the sweet smell of the beautiful flowers and the good taste of the food God made for them. Adam and Eve had everything they needed. But they had something else too—they had God as their best friend. When they heard the leaves of the trees moving in a soft rustling sound, they knew that God was nearby.

One day when Eve was by herself, a snake came up to her and asked, "Has God told you not to eat the fruit from any of the trees in the garden?"

"Oh, Adam and I may eat the fruit from all the trees in the garden except one," Eve told the snake. "God told us not to touch the tree in the middle of the garden and not to eat any of its fruit. If we do, we will die."

"Oh, no!" said the snake. "You will not die. God does not want you to eat the fruit of that tree because He knows it will make you as smart as He is."

The snake said that God had lied to Adam and Eve, but God cannot lie. The snake had lied, and Eve believed the snake. She looked at the tree in the middle of the garden. The fruit looked good to her. Eve thought about how smart she would be. So she disobeyed God and ate some of the fruit. Then she gave some to Adam, and he ate it, too.

Adam and Eve did the one thing that God had told

them not to do. And now they felt so bad. They tried to hide from God. But God called out to Adam, "Where are you?"

Adam said, "I was afraid for You to see me."

"Why were you afraid?" God asked. "Did you eat from the tree in the middle of the garden?"

Then Adam told God that Eve had caused him to eat the fruit. And Eve said the snake had told her to eat it. But it was no use. God knew the truth.

Now God had to punish Adam and Eve and the snake. He told the snake, "You will have to crawl on your belly in the dirt all of your life." And He told Adam and Eve, "You will have to leave this beautiful garden now, and your life won't be as happy as it was here."

Then God gave Adam and Eve coats of animal skins and sent them out of the garden. Their lives would never be the same. But God still loved Adam and Eve. He cared about them very much and gave them a special blessing—a baby boy. They named him Cain. Later God let them have another baby boy, and his name was Abel.

God's Special Helpers

A Boat, a Flood, and a Promise

God had made the earth just right for people, and He wanted people to love each other and be kind. But instead, people were hurting and killing each other.

God felt very sad. He said, "I am sorry I made people. I am going to destroy them and all my other creatures, and start all over."

But God found one good man. His name was Noah. Noah was kind to other people and obeyed God.

God told Noah how he would be saved. He said, "Build a big boat of gopher wood. Make rooms in it. Make three decks, and cover it with pitch so water can't get in. Build a door in the side and make one window."

God told Noah, "I am going to flood the earth with water and destroy all living things. But I will make a special promise to you and your wife and your sons, Shem, Ham, and Japheth and their wives. I promise that all of you will be saved." God planned to begin a new world of people with Noah's family.

God also had plans for the animals, birds, and fish. God told Noah to take pairs, which means two, of each kind of His creatures into the big boat. He said to take one pair of some kinds of animals and seven pairs of others. Then the animals would be saved, too.

Noah worked very hard to build the ark. It took a long time, and the wicked people made fun of Noah and laughed at him. But Noah kept building the ark. And when the boat was finished, Noah and his family took all of the animals and led them into the ark. Last of all,

Noah and his family went inside, and God shut the door.

After seven days, everyone in the ark heard the sound of rain—hard rain. Day after day, the rain fell. The water rose and flooded the earth and made the ark float on top of it. The rain fell on the earth for forty days and forty nights without stopping. Every living thing died, and the water rose so high that it covered the mountains.

But God did not forget Noah and his family and the animals in the ark. God caused a strong wind to blow and begin drying the earth. The water began to go back into the lakes and seas and rivers. Then Noah's ark stopped floating and came to rest on the top of a tall mountain called Ararat.

Forty days after the ark stopped moving, Noah opened the window and no water came in. He took a raven and let it fly out. The raven did not come back. Then Noah let a dove fly out the window. The dove flew around but couldn't find a place to live because of the water, so she came back to the ark. She landed on Noah's hand.

After a week, Noah sent the dove out again. This time the dove brought an olive leaf back in her beak. Noah knew the water was lower. After seven more days, Noah sent the dove out again. This time, she did not return to the ark. She had found a home.

Then God told Noah, "You and your family may leave the ark. Take the animals and birds with you. I want the earth to have more people, more animals, and more birds. I want it to be beautiful and full of life again."

Then God promised never to destroy the earth with a big flood again. And to remind us of His promise, God put a rainbow in the sky.

God Blesses Abraham

God loved His people, and He had special plans for them. One of the men God had special plans for was Abram. God told Abram, "I want you to leave your country and your father's family and go to a land that I will show you. And I will make you very happy. You will have a big family, and be a great person. Then someday, someone from your family will make all of the families in the world happy."

Abram loved God and did just what God told him to do. Abram took his wife, Sarah, and his nephew, Lot, and everything they owned and started to go to the land of Canaan.

God said, "I will give this land to your family." Abram was so thankful that he built an altar and thanked God.

Abram and Sarah and Lot and the people who worked

for them traveled some more. Then they came to a place called Bethel and pitched their tents. There Abram built another altar and prayed to God, because God was helping him.

God had promised Abram that he would have a big family with many grandchildren, great grandchildren, and great-great grandchildren. More and more children would be born as the years passed. God said, "There will be as many people in your family as there are grains of sand on the seashore and stars in the sky. And from now on your name will be Abraham."

Abraham believed God, but he and Sarah were getting old, and they still didn't have a child. But God always keeps His promises. And soon Sarah had a son. They named him Isaac. Sarah and Abraham knew that God would bless Isaac. He would keep His promises to Isaac as He had to them.

A Wife for Isaac

Abraham was one of the happiest people on earth. God had given him everything he needed and wanted. God also had promised Abraham that he would have a large family with many grandchildren, great grandchildren, great-great grandchildren, and on and on through the years.

Abraham knew that it was time to choose a wife for his son, Isaac. So he told his oldest and best servant exactly how to choose a wife for Isaac. "Go back to the land where I used to live," Abraham said. "Take gifts and listen to God. He will help you know who will make a good wife for Isaac."

The good servant obeyed Abraham. He took ten camels and gold and silver jewelry and beautiful cloth. When he got to the city where Abraham's brother lived, he stopped and prayed, "Lord, God of Abraham, I am going to wait by this well of water until You show me the woman you want to be Isaac's wife. So I'll know which one she is, let her be the one who gives me a drink of water and then gives a drink to my camels also."

The servant waited until a pretty woman named Rebekah came to the spring to get water. When she had filled her jar, he said to her, "Will you please let me drink a little water from your jar?"

"Drink, sir," Rebekah said. And she quickly gave him a drink of water. Then Rebekah said, "I will give your camels water, too, until they have had enough to drink."

The servant was excited. He gave Rebekah a gold ring and two gold bracelets. Then he asked her, "Who is your father? And does he have room for me and the people with me to stay at his house tonight?"

"I am Bethuel's daughter," Rebekah told him, "and we have plenty of room for you and your camels."

Then the servant knew that God had answered his prayer. "Thank you, God," he prayed, "for leading me to the house of Abraham's brothers."

Soon Rebekah and her servants started back with Abraham's servant to where Isaac lived. As they came near, Isaac was in a field watching them. He saw Rebekah riding a camel and came to meet them.

When Rebekah saw Isaac, she got off her camel and asked the servant, "Who is he?"

"He is my master, Isaac," the servant answered.

When Rebekah and Abraham's servant got to Isaac, the servant told him everything that had happened. Isaac was pleased. He married Rebekah and was very happy.

A Stone Pillow
and a Special Dream

Jacob was running away from home. But he wasn't a little boy; he was a grown man. Jacob was leaving his parents, Isaac and Rebekah, because his brother, Esau, was very angry with him. Esau was so angry at something Jacob had done to him, that he had said, "I want to kill Jacob."

Jacob's mother told him, "You must leave at once and go to the country where your uncle, Laban, lives. Stay there until your brother, Esau, isn't angry anymore. I will tell you when to come home."

And Jacob's father, Isaac, said to him, "While you are at Laban's house, you should choose a wife."

Then Isaac who was old and blind prayed a special prayer for his son, Jacob. He said, "May God give you a big family, and may He give the blessing to you that He gave to your grandfather, Abraham. May God give the land He promised to Abraham to you and your children and grandchildren."

Then Jacob left his father and mother and went to a different country. Jacob traveled a long way, and he probably traveled as fast as he could because he was afraid of his brother, Esau. That night Jacob was very tired. He took a stone and put it under his head for a pillow. Soon he was fast asleep.

While Jacob slept, he had a dream. He saw a ladder that stretched all the way from earth to Heaven. And angels of God were walking up and down the ladder.

God spoke to Jacob in the dream and said, "I am the Lord. I am the God of Abraham and the God of Isaac. The land on which you are sleeping will belong to you and your children and their children. You will have a very large family, and someone in your family will bring good news to everyone on earth.

God made another promise to Jacob. He said, "I am with you, and I will take care of you and bring you back to this land. I will keep my promise."

When Jacob awoke, he said, "This is a very special place because God was here. I will set up this stone that I used for a pillow to remind me that God spoke to me here."

So Jacob set the stone up, poured oil on the top of it and called the place Bethel, which means "The house of God." Then he continued on his journey to his uncle's house, but he never forgot the wonderful dream.

Joseph and His Brothers

Joseph's brothers were jealous of him because their father loved Joseph more than them. Jacob loved all of his sons, but because he loved Joseph the most, he gave him a special coat of beautiful colors. And when the brothers saw Joseph coming, wearing his special coat, it made them so angry they wanted to kill him.

"No! Let's not kill him," said Reuben. "Let's just throw him into a pit." Reuben planned to come back later and get Joseph out of the pit.

So the brothers took his beautiful coat and threw Joseph into a big hole. Then they sat down to eat.

While Reuben was away from the other brothers, Judah said, "See that group of men with their camels? They are going down to Egypt. Let's sell Joseph to them. Let's not kill him since he is our brother." So they sold Joseph to the traders who took him to Egypt.

Later, Reuben came back to the pit. But Joseph was not there. *"Oh, no!"* Reuben thought, *"Joseph is gone. What am I going to tell our father?"*

His brothers said, "Let's kill a goat and put its blood on Joseph's coat and tell our father a wild animal killed him." They did, and when their father, Jacob, saw the coat, he believed that Joseph was dead.

In Egypt, Joseph was far away from home, but God was watching over him. And Joseph was very smart. He could even explain the meanings of dreams with God's help. And when the Pharaoh told two of his dreams to Joseph, Joseph said, "Your dreams mean that for seven years the farmers in Egypt will grow good crops. Everyone will have plenty of food. Then for the next seven years, the farmers will not be able to grow good crops.

There will not be enough food in Egypt. And you should choose someone to be in charge of saving food, now, so the people will not starve when the bad years come."

The Pharaoh chose Joseph for this job, and Joseph saved lots of grain during the seven good years. And when the seven bad years came, all of the people of Egypt had food to eat.

And way back in the land where Joseph used to live, his father and brothers did not have enough food to eat. So Jacob said to his sons, "I have heard that there is food in Egypt. Go there and buy some for us."

So Jacob's sons went down to Egypt to buy grain. They didn't know that the man who sold it to them was their brother, Joseph. But Joseph knew them, and he was very glad to see his brothers. But he didn't tell them who he was.

When Joseph learned that his father and youngest brother, Benjamin, were still alive, he said, "I will keep Simeon in prison until you go back home and return with your youngest brother. Then I will know you are not spies."

When Joseph's brothers went home and told their father what the man in Egypt had said, he was sad. But when their food was gone, Jacob sent them to Egypt again—this time with their brother, Benjamin.

And when Joseph saw Benjamin, he told them, "I am your brother, Joseph, whom you sold into slavery. But God wanted me to be in Egypt so I could save your lives."

Joseph's brothers could hardly believe what he told them. And Joseph was so happy to see Benjamin that he hugged him and cried and cried. Then he said, "Go home and bring our father and your families back to Egypt. All of you can live here and have everything you need."

A Baby in the Bulrushes

"Shh! Don't cry," Jochebed said, as she looked at her beautiful baby boy. She was sad because the wicked, mean ruler of Egypt, the Pharaoh, wanted to kill her baby. He wanted to kill all the Hebrew boy babies as soon as they were born. Jochebed loved her baby and didn't want him killed. So she hid him in her house.

Jochebed thought as she watched her little boy sleep, "I cannot hide him much longer. He cries louder now, and one of the Egyptians could hear him. If the bad Pharaoh hears him, he will have him killed."

So Jochebed said, "Miriam, I know what I am going to do. I will make a little basket-boat and put your brother in it. Then I'll ask God to protect him."

Jochebed made the boat and put her little boy in it. Then she carried the basket-boat down to the river. It floated on top of the water where the tall bulrushes grew. Miriam hid where no one could see her and watched the basket.

Soon Miriam saw someone coming to the river to take a bath. It was a princess, the Pharaoh's own daughter! And when the princess saw the basket-boat, she said to her maids, "I see a basket. Bring it to me." Then the princess looked inside, and saw the beautiful little boy.

"I'll keep this little Hebrew baby," the princess said. And she named him Moses.

Then Miriam came to the princess and said, "May I get one of the Hebrew women to care for this baby for you?"

The princess said yes, and Miriam ran as fast as she could to get her mother, Jochebed!

God's
Special People

Moses Leads God's People

The people of Israel lived in Egypt a long time. They worked very hard, but the harder they worked, the meaner the Egyptians were to them.

When Moses grew to be a man, he saw how unhappy the Israelites were. They had been made slaves to the Egyptians, and it made him angry and sad. But God had a special way for Moses to help his people.

God had heard the cries of the Israelite people as they begged Him to help them. So God chose Moses to lead the Israelites out of Egypt.

Moses went to the Pharaoh and asked him to let the Israelite people leave Egypt. Pharaoh kept saying no. So God punished the Egyptians with bad things called plagues. First, He turned their river to blood so they could not drink it or wash in it, but even then Pharaoh would not let the people go.

Then God sent millions of frogs to hop all over Egypt—even in the houses, but still Pharaoh would not let the Israelites leave.

God punished the Egyptians ten different times with bad plagues. Sometimes Pharaoh would say, "Yes, you may leave," but when the bad things were over, he would change his mind.

Finally, God sent one last terrible punishment on the Egyptians. God knew this last bad thing would be sure to make Pharaoh let the people leave. So God had Moses tell the Israelites to get ready to leave.

And that night, God sent His death angel to every Egyptian home and the oldest son died. But no one died in the homes of the Israelites, because God had told them what to do. And just as God had said, Pharaoh let the Israelites leave Egypt.

Crossing the Red Sea

"Get out of my land!" Pharaoh told Moses. "You and all of the children of Israel, leave now!"

Moses did not wait. He told the Israelites, "Let's go now. Pharaoh is finally letting us leave."

So they left Egypt—thousands and thousands of Israelite men, women, and children and all of their animals. They followed Moses to the Red Sea. Then God told them to camp beside the sea.

But back in Egypt, the wicked Pharaoh was changing his mind again. *"What have we done?"* he asked himself. *"Who will work for us now that the Israelites are gone? We must go after them and bring them back."*

So the Pharaoh and his army rode after the Israelites. There were soldiers riding horses and soldiers marching. They kept going until they could see the Israelites camped by the Red Sea.

When the men and women with Moses saw the Egyptians coming, they were afraid.

"Why did you lead us here, Moses?" they asked. "We should have stayed in Egypt and died there. We don't want to die here."

But Moses trusted God, and he told the people, "Don't be afraid. God will save you today."

Then God said to Moses, "Stretch your hand over the sea and divide it. The people of Israel will walk through on dry land." And they did!

When the Egyptians saw the Israelites walking through the sea, they started to follow. But God had a plan. He told Moses, "Stretch out your hand over the sea again and make the waters come back together."

Moses obeyed God, and all of the Egyptians were drowned in the Red Sea that day.

Rules for God's People

God's people needed two things to help them become a good nation. They needed to know how to worship and obey God, and how to treat other people.

Moses told everyone, "Wash your clothes so that you will be clean, because in three days God is going to come down to the top of this mountain. And God said that you must not touch the mountain or even come close to it."

The Israelites did everything Moses told them, and three days later God came to the top of Mount Sinai in the morning. No one could see God because the mountain was covered by a thick cloud. There was thunder and flashes of lightning. Then a trumpet sounded so loud that all of the people shook with fear.

Moses and the Israelites waited at the bottom of the mountain. When the sounds of the trumpet grew louder and louder, Moses spoke, and God answered him with a voice that boomed like thunder. Then God called Moses to come up to the top of the mountain. There God told Moses to warn the people not to come near the mountain because God would be too bright and shiny for them to look at. So Moses went back down from the mountain and warned the people not to come near the mountain while God was there.

Then the people moved farther back from the mountain. They watched Moses go up, up, up again into the thick cloud that covered the mountain where God was.

Moses was on the mountain with God a long time. When he came down, he brought stone tablets with ten special laws written on them. We call these ten special laws, the Ten Commandments.

The Promised Land

"Here they come!" said the excited men and women. "Joshua and Caleb and the other spies are back from Canaan."

Twelve men had gone into the Promised Land to do a very important job. Moses had told them, "See if the land is good or bad. See what the people are like. Come back and tell me if the cities are open or have walls around them. And tell me if the land is good for growing crops."

Everyone wanted to hear what the men had to say. First, they had some good news.

"It is a good land for growing crops. Just look at this fruit," they said. The grapes were so big that it took two men to carry one bunch between them on a pole.

But what about the people in Canaan, everyone wanted to know. And the spies told them, "The people who live in Canaan are big and strong. They live in big cities with walls around them."

When the people heard this, they were afraid. They began to worry and complain. But Joshua and Caleb, two of the spies, said, "We can take this land and live in it. If God is pleased with us, He will help us take this land."

God was sorry that the people were afraid to go into the land He had promised to give them. So God said that the people who were afraid would wander in the wilderness for forty years—until they all grew old and died. They would not get to live in Canaan.

God also said, "Joshua and Caleb will get to go into the Promised Land of Canaan, because they gave a good report and because they believed in me."

The Walls of Jericho

After Moses died, God said to Joshua, "It is now time for the people of Israel to go into the land I have promised them. Be strong and don't be afraid."

Now Joshua knew that his armies would have to take the land away from the people who lived there. So Joshua sent two spies to visit the city of Jericho. He told them to see what the land was like, and then come back and tell him.

When the spies returned to Joshua after three days, they said, "God has given us this land. The people who live there are afraid of us."

Later, God told Joshua exactly how to take over the city of Jericho. God said that some of Joshua's soldiers should line up and march around the city. They were to be followed by seven priests carrying trumpets and other priests carrying the ark of the covenant.

Then Joshua told everyone, "Do not say a word until I tell you. We will march quietly around the city of Jericho for seven days. Then on the seventh day when I tell you to shout, shout as loud as you can."

For six days the soldiers and priests marched all the way around the city of Jericho, one time each day. The priests blew their trumpets the whole time. The people inside Jericho were afraid. They did not dare to go outside. They wondered what would happen next.

On the seventh day, the soldiers and the priests carrying the ark of God's covenant marched around the city seven times. And then when the other priests blew their trumpets, Joshua told the people, "Shout!" The people shouted as loud as they could, and the walls of Jericho fell down flat.

Hannah Trusted God

Every year Hannah and her husband, Elkanah, went to God's house, the tabernacle, to worship God at a special service. But every year when it was time to eat the special meal, Hannah would be so sad she couldn't eat.

Elkanah knew that his wife, Hannah, wanted a son more than anything else in the world. She wanted to be a mother, but she had no children.

"I know what I am going to do," Hannah said to herself. *"I will make a special promise to God when I pray."*

When the meal was over, Hannah went to the big tent to pray. She was so sad when she prayed that she was crying very hard. Her lips moved as she talked to God in Heaven, but she didn't say any words out loud.

And this is what Hannah prayed, "O God of hosts, if you will give me a son, I will give him back to You for all of his life. To show that he is a special gift for You, I will never cut his hair." Hannah prayed a long time.

Eli, the priest, said to Hannah, "Go in peace, and may God give you what you have asked for."

Hannah and Elkanah got up early the next morning and worshiped God again. Then they went back home.

After awhile, Hannah's prayer was answered. A baby boy was born to her and her husband, and they named him Samuel. Hannah was very happy. She stayed home and took care of Samuel.

And when Samuel was a young boy, Hannah did what she had promised. She took Samuel to Eli the priest and said, "I am the woman who prayed for a son. God answered my prayer. Here is the boy God gave me. I have brought him to live with you here and to serve God the rest of his life."

45

Choosing a King

Samuel was now an old man. He had been telling the people to obey God's laws and helping them when they had problems for many years. He had served God from the time his mother, Hannah, had brought him to God's house when he was a little boy.

One day the leaders of the Israelites came to Samuel with an idea. "We want a king to rule us," they said.

"Why do you want a king?" Samuel asked.

"We want to be like the other nations around us," the men said. "If we have a king to lead us, we will win all of the battles we fight."

Samuel listened to everything the men had to say, and he did not like their idea. But he prayed to God about it, and God told him, "Don't be angry with them, Samuel. But be sure they know what it will be like to have a king."

Samuel told the people, "A king will want you to work for him and give him presents."

"We still want a king," the people answered Samuel.

Then God said, "Give them a king."

So Samuel called all of the tribes of Israel together, and then he chose the tribe of Benjamin. He knew that the king God had chosen was in that family. Samuel asked for Saul, the son of Kish, to step forward.

"Where is Saul?" the people asked. But the new king was shy. He was hiding. So the people ran and got Saul and stood him in front of everyone.

Samuel said, "Look at the man God has chosen to be your king. There is no one like him."

To show that God had chosen Saul to be the king of Israel, Samuel poured drops of oil on his head.

A Boy Meets a Giant

David was excited. He was going to the battlefield where the army of Israel was facing the army of the Philistines. The young shepherd boy was going to take food to his three older brothers who were in the army of Israel.

"Come back and tell me how your brothers are," Jesse told his son.

"I will," David said, and hurried away.

As David got close to the valley where the army of Israel was, he heard a loud voice coming from one of the mountains.

"Why do you come to fight us in a battle?" the voice shouted to the army of Israel. "Just send someone to fight me. If he kills me, then the Philistines will serve you. But if I kill him, then you will serve us."

As David got closer, he could see the man standing on a mountain across the valley. It was Goliath, a man almost ten feet tall. David had never seen anyone so big! He was a giant!

Again Goliath yelled to the Israelite army, "I dare you, army of Israel. Send one of your soldiers to fight me today." But no one wanted to fight Goliath. They were all too afraid. When King Saul and the whole army of Israel heard Goliath, they shook with fear.

For forty days, Goliath had been shouting across the valley to the army of Israel, "Send someone to fight me." And for forty days no one had gone to fight him.

When David got to the Israelite army's camp, he went to King Saul and said, "No one should be afraid because of Goliath. I will go and fight him."

"But you are too young," the king told David. "Goliath

has been a soldier for a long time. He knows how to fight better than you do."

Then David answered, "When I was taking care of my father's sheep, I killed both a lion and a bear to protect them. And I will kill this Philistine, too."

Saul knew how much David trusted God, so he said, "Go and fight the giant, and may God be with you and help you."

King Saul gave David a helmet to protect his head and armor to protect his body. But David wasn't used to wearing them, and he took them off. David did not even take a sword to fight Goliath. Instead, he chose special weapons—a big stick, his sling, and five smooth stones from a creek. David put the stones into his shepherd's pouch and walked toward the battle line.

Goliath was wearing heavy armor and a man was carrying a shield in front of him. Goliath looked down at David. He laughed and made fun of him, but David wasn't afraid.

David said, "You come to me with a sword and a spear, but I come to you in the name of the Lord, the God of the armies of Israel. You made fun of God, but today He will help me kill you, and I will cut your head off. Then everyone will know that God leads Israel."

Goliath did not like David's brave words, and he moved forward toward him. Quickly, David ran forward toward Goliath. He put a stone into his sling and sent it flying through the air. The stone struck Goliath in the forehead. It sank deep into Goliath's head and killed him, and he fell on the ground.

Then David ran and took the giant's own sword and cut his head off with it. Now the Philistines were afraid. They ran away, and the army of Israel ran after them and won the battle.

Good Friends

David and Jonathan became good friends the first time they met. Jonathan was a prince, the son of King Saul. And David was a shepherd, tending his father's sheep.

Jonathan said to David, "I will be your friend always. To prove that I am your friend, I will give you my very own robe, my armor, my bow and arrows, and my belt."

David liked Jonathan, too, and they promised each other to be good friends always. But King Saul was not a good friend of David's. He was jealous of David, because David was such a good soldier.

David was afraid of King Saul, and so he ran away. But first he talked to Jonathan and said, "Let me know if your father, the king, plans to kill me."

"I will," Jonathan said. "But you must go away and hide for three days in our secret place. And I will find out if my father is still angry with you. Then I will come to the place where you are hiding and shoot arrows. I will bring a young boy with me to get the arrows I shoot. If I say to him, 'The arrows are beyond you,' then you will know that my father wants to kill you."

In three days, Jonathan and a little boy came to the field where David was hiding. Jonathan shot an arrow, and David heard him say to the boy, "Isn't the arrow beyond you?"

David was sorry to hear Jonathan say that. It meant that King Saul wanted to kill him.

Then David came out from his hiding place. And the two good friends kissed each other and cried, because David would have to keep running away from King Saul. They didn't know if they would ever see each other again.

A Song of David

David was a shepherd, a soldier, and a king. And David played a harp and sang songs. All of his life, David sang songs to tell God how he felt. Some of his songs are written in the Bible in the book of Psalms. Here is one of the songs David wrote.

O God, our God,
    How wonderful is your name everywhere on the earth.
We can see your greatness in the skies.
    Even young children know how great you are.

When I think about the heavens You made with Your hands,
And the moon and the stars that you put in their places.
I wonder why you made men and women and why You care for us.
But You have made men and women very special.
    You have made them beautiful and important.

You created men and women to take care of the earth.
You have made them greater than Your other creations.
Greater than the sheep, the cows, all of the animals.
    Greater than the birds in the sky, the fish in the seas,
Whatever creature lives in the water.
    O God, our God,
How wonderful is your name all over the earth.

—Adapted from Psalm 8

Building God's Temple

King Solomon was a good and wise king. One day he said, "I am going to build a house of worship for God. When my father, King David, wanted to build a temple for God, God told him, 'Your son will build it. You, David, cannot build it because of all of the wars going on.'"

Solomon said, "Now there is no fighting. The land is peaceful, so I am going to build God's house."

And Solomon wanted the best of everything for God's house. So he asked for the very best workers and the very best materials—special stones, cedar and fir and olive wood, gold and brass. Smart men from other countries helped make the special carvings and furniture and dishes for God's house. Everyone worked very hard.

Because the temple was to be God's special house, everyone worked quietly around it. They did their noisy work, like sawing wood and cutting stones, away from the temple. Then they brought the wood and the big stones to Jerusalem and put them in place.

Solomon had special gold and silver bowls that his father, David, had saved for God's house. And the priests carried the most special piece of furniture for God's house—the ark of the covenant. Inside it were the stone tablets with the Ten Commandments that God had given to Moses hundreds of years before.

It took seven years to build the temple. When it was finished, Solomon called all of the men and women and children together to dedicate it to God. The people were very quiet.

King Solomon prayed a long prayer, asking God to bless the people in every way.

A Young Girl Helps Naaman

Naaman was an important man. He was the captain of the army of the king of Syria. But Naaman had a problem. He had a sickness called leprosy that caused bad sores on his skin. And no one had been able to help him get well.

But there was someone who knew how Naaman could be healed of his leprosy—a young Israelite girl who worked for Naaman's wife. She said, "If Naaman would go see God's prophet in Samaria, he would make him well."

Naaman wanted to be made well more than anything. So he hurried in his chariot to Elisha's house.

But Elisha didn't even come out of his house and talk to Naaman. Instead, he sent a message to Naaman telling him to do something strange. Elisha said, "Go to the Jordan River and wash yourself seven times. Then your skin will be healed, and your leprosy will be gone."

Naaman was angry. He was so angry that he left Elisha's house.

Naaman started to go home, but his servants said to him, "The prophet asked you to do something easy, just wash in the Jordan River seven times. Why don't you do it?" Naaman thought about it. Then he said to himself, *"Yes, I will do it."*

He went to the Jordan River and dipped himself in it seven times. The first six times, nothing happened. But when he came out of the water the seventh time, his skin was perfect. All of the sores were gone. He was well!

Naaman was so happy that he and his friends rode their chariots back to Elisha's house and thanked him.

Daniel in the Lions' Den

Daniel had been taken to a faraway country when he was a young man. But Daniel obeyed the laws of God even though he was away from home. He prayed to God three times a day.

King Darius, the ruler of the country where he now lived, gave Daniel a very important job. But the men who worked for Daniel were jealous of him.

"Let's get rid of Daniel," they said.

Then the men went to King Darius and had him pass a law. The law said that anyone who prayed to any god or man, but the king himself, for thirty days, would be thrown into the lions' den.

Daniel refused to obey the king's new law. He loved God more than anyone else. So he went into his house and got down on his knees to pray as he always had.

The men hurried to tell the king, "Daniel is still praying to his God three times a day."

Now, King Darius was sorry he had made the law. He wanted to change it, but the bad men reminded him that no law could be changed. So Daniel was put in the den with the hungry lions.

That night the king was so worried about Daniel, he couldn't eat or sleep. And as soon as the sun came up the next morning, King Darius hurried to the lions' den and called out, "Daniel! Has your God saved you?"

"Oh, yes, King Darius," Daniel answered. "God sent an angel to close the lions' mouths."

King Darius was so happy, he made a new law that everyone should worship the God who had saved Daniel from the lions. Then the king had the bad men themselves put into the lions' den!

God's Special Son

Good News!

Zacharias, the priest, was excited. It was his turn to serve God in the temple. Zacharias' job was to burn incense at a special altar while the people who came to worship stood outside and prayed.

Zacharias entered the special room in the temple and burned the sweet-smelling incense as an offering to God. This was a moment Zacharias had waited for all his life. But something he didn't expect happened. As Zacharias burned the incense, an angel of God stood by the altar. Zacharias was very surprised and afraid.

But the angel said, "Don't be afraid, Zacharias. God has heard your prayer. You and your wife, Elizabeth, are going to have a little baby boy. You will name your little boy John. Many people will be happy that John is born. He will be a special helper for God. Many people will obey God when they hear John preach."

Zacharias didn't know what to think. "This is hard to believe," he told the angel. "My wife and I are old. How can I be sure this will happen?"

"I am Gabriel who stands in the presence of God," the angel answered. "I have been sent to tell you this good news. But because you have not believed my words, you will not be able to talk until these things happen."

Now Zacharias had been in the temple a long time. The crowd of people outside wondered what had happened to him. But when he came out, he could not tell them because he was not able to talk.

When Zacharias finished his work at the temple, he went home to the place where he and his wife, Elizabeth, lived. Several months later, just as Gabriel told him, their baby boy was born.

Elizabeth's relatives and friends were very happy for her. They knew God had blessed her in a special way, because she had been waiting so long for a baby. When the baby was eight days old, relatives and friends of Zacharias and Elizabeth came for a special service for the baby. They wanted to name him Zacharias like his father, but Elizabeth said, "No! He will be called John."

The men and women were surprised. "But no one in your family is named John," they said to Elizabeth. Then they made signs to Zacharias, who still could not talk, to find out what he wanted to name the baby. Zacharias motioned for a tablet and wrote, "His name is John." Everyone was surprised.

Then everyone had a bigger surprise because at that moment, Zacharias could talk. His very first words were words of praise to God. Zacharias was very happy.

The friends and relatives remembered Zacharias' words and talked about them for a long time. They wondered, "What kind of man will this child John be? God must surely be with him." And they were right.

An Angel Visits Mary

Several months after the angel Gabriel appeared to Zacharias in the temple, God sent him with a special message to a young woman named Mary.

"Hello, Mary," Gabriel said, "God is pleased with you, and He wants you to do something special for Him."

Mary was frightened. She hadn't seen an angel before, and she didn't know what Gabriel meant.

"Don't be afraid, Mary," the angel said. "God has sent me to tell you that you are going to have a baby boy. You will name Him Jesus. He will be the most special baby ever born because He will be God's own Son."

"How can this happen to me?" Mary asked the angel. "I don't have a husband. I'm not married to Joseph yet."

Then Gabriel told her, "God will make this miracle happen. He will bless you as He has blessed your cousin, Elizabeth. In a few months, she will have a baby too, even though she is much too old. Wonderful things are possible with God's help."

Mary believed the angel. She said, "I love God and want to serve Him. I will do whatever He wants me to do." Then the angel left.

Mary was surprised and pleased that God had chosen her to have this special baby. And she was also very happy for her cousin, Elizabeth. So Mary decided to go visit Elizabeth and tell her what the angel had said.

God's Spirit told Elizabeth that Mary was going to be the mother of Jesus. This news made Elizabeth very excited and happy. And when Mary came into Elizabeth's house she said, "Hello, Elizabeth."

Elizabeth answered, "I am so glad you have come, Mary, because you are going to be the mother of Jesus."

Jesus Is Born

The road from Nazareth to Bethlehem was long. Mary and Joseph traveled slowly. Every once in a while, Joseph probably asked, "Are you tired, Mary?"

"A little," she may have said. "I think the baby will be born soon."

"Then we'll rest awhile," Joseph told her. It probably took them a few days to travel from Nazareth to Bethlehem. They had to go up and down many hills. But finally they reached Bethlehem, the city of David.

"There are so many people here in Bethlehem," Joseph said, "that we may have trouble finding a room." And they did. Mary and Joseph couldn't find any place to stay. Then someone, perhaps a kind innkeeper, let them stay in a stable. The animals didn't mind, and Mary and Joseph were so happy to have a place to sleep.

But they couldn't sleep that night because something very exciting happened. A baby boy was born to Mary, just as the angel Gabriel had promised. Mary wrapped the baby in cloth and laid Him on a bed of hay in a manger. She named Him, Jesus.

That night as the lamps flickered in the windows of Bethlehem, stars shone down on shepherds watching their sheep in a field nearby. Perhaps a shepherd boy played his flute softly, while the sheep made low "baa-ing" sounds. Some of the sheep and shepherds were asleep.

Suddenly the shepherds were startled by a bright light from the sky. Then an angel appeared to them, and they were frightened.

"Don't be afraid," the angel told the shepherds. "I have good news for you that will bring a lot of happiness to everyone. A baby has just been born in Bethlehem. And this baby is the Son of God."

The shepherds listened closely as the angel told them where they could find the baby.

"He is in a stable in Bethlehem, sleeping in a manger on some hay," said the angel.

Then suddenly, there were many angels praising God and saying, "Glory to God in the highest, and on earth, peace to men and women because God wants to make them happy."

As soon as the angels left, the shepherds said, "Let's go to Bethlehem right now and see this baby that the angels have told us about."

So the shepherds hurried and found Mary and Joseph and baby Jesus. Jesus was wrapped in cloths and lying in a manger filled with hay. They knew this must be the right baby, and so the shepherds told Mary and Joseph what the angel had told them.

Mary and Joseph were glad the shepherds had come. They were glad to hear what the angel had told them about Jesus. Mary thought about what the shepherds told her. Perhaps she was thinking, too, about Gabriel's visit to her months before.

The shepherds went back to their flocks, praising God and thanking Him for leading them to Jesus, His Son.

Wise-men Worship Jesus

After Jesus had been born in Bethlehem, some men who studied the stars came looking for Him. They lived far away in the east. These men were not sure where to find Jesus, so they went to Jerusalem. They stopped everyone they met and asked, "Where can we find the King of the Jews? We saw His star shining in the east, and we have come to worship Him." But no one seemed to know where Jesus was.

When King Herod heard that there were men from the east looking for another king, he got very angry. Herod didn't want anyone else to be king. And the people in Jerusalem were worried, too. They didn't know what King Herod might do.

And King Herod did have a plan. He called all the religious leaders and teachers together and asked, "Where will the King of the Jews be born?" They looked in the Bible and found the words of the prophet Micah who wrote that a ruler or king would be born "in Bethlehem."

Then King Herod pretended that he wanted to help the Wise-men find Jesus. So he asked them, "When did you first see the star?" They told him. Then Herod said, "Look for Him in Bethlehem, and when you find Him, come back and tell me exactly where He is. I want to go and worship Him, too."

So the Wise-men left King Herod and started toward Bethlehem. And when they looked up into the sky, they saw the beautiful star. It was the same star they had seen in their own country far away. The Wise-men were happy to see the star. Now they knew for certain that God was leading them in the right direction.

The star moved and led the Wise-men to the exact house where Jesus and His parents were. Then it stopped. Its beams shone down on the house to let the Wise-men know, "Here is where you'll find the baby King."

The Wise-men entered the house and saw Mary and Jesus. They kneeled and worshiped Him. And when they finished worshiping Jesus, they gave Him their gifts—gold, frankincense and myrrh. The Wise-men had brought expensive gifts because they were for a King.

Before the Wise-men left Bethlehem to go back home, God warned them in a special dream, *"Do not tell King Herod where Jesus is. He is mean and wants to kill Him. Go back to your homes by a road that does not go to Jerusalem where King Herod lives."*

Jesus' Special Work

A Special Trip

While Jesus was still a baby, Mary and Joseph took Him back to Nazareth where they had lived. Jesus was a good son. Whatever Mary asked Jesus to do, He was glad to do. Perhaps Jesus helped Joseph in his carpenter's shop, too.

Jesus played with His friends in the streets of Nazareth. He learned a lot of Bible verses from Joseph and Mary, too.

When Jesus was twelve years old, He was old enough to worship with the men in the temple at Jerusalem. Joseph and Mary went to the temple every year to remember the Passover, and Jesus was eager to go. The trip took about three days, but it was fun because so many men and women, boys and girls were going from Nazareth and other cities. The people did not want to miss worshiping God in the temple. At the Passover feast, the Jewish people remembered how God helped Moses lead them out of Egypt many years before. This was a way of saying thank you to God.

Thousands of people lived in the city of Jerusalem. Many of them opened their homes to the families who came from far away.

In the homes, the families ate the Passover meal and read Scriptures. At the temple, the men and boys offered their sacrifices.

When the Passover celebration was finished, Mary and Joseph started home to Nazareth, along with the other families. They must have thought Jesus was in the group somewhere. But He wasn't!

After Mary and Joseph and the others had been traveling back home for one day, Mary looked for Jesus.

He wasn't with her friends or family. Perhaps she thought, *"He is with Joseph and the men."*

Then Joseph looked for Jesus and didn't see Him either. Maybe he thought, *"He is probably with His mother or some of the other children."*

But that evening, when Mary and Joseph stopped to rest, they said to each other, "Where is Jesus? I thought He was with you."

Then they asked the people traveling with them, but no one had seen Jesus. Now they knew that He was missing!

The next day Mary and Joseph went all the way back to Jerusalem. They were worried. Perhaps they thought, *"This isn't like Jesus. He always obeys, and He is always where He is supposed to be."*

In Jerusalem they looked everywhere and asked everyone they saw, "Have you seen our boy, Jesus?" But no one had.

Then the third day, Mary and Joseph found Jesus. They found Him in the temple, talking to some of the teachers of God's Word. Jesus was listening to what the teachers had to say and asking them questions. These men were very, very smart, and they were surprised at how much this twelve-year-old boy understood about God and the Bible.

Mary and Joseph were thankful they had found Jesus, but Mary scolded Him, "Son, why did you do this? Your father and I have looked everywhere for you."

Jesus answered, "Didn't you know that I had to be in my Father's house?" Jesus meant God's house, the temple, because He is God's Son.

Then Jesus went home to Nazareth with Mary and Joseph. He obeyed them, and continued to grow and learn in a way that pleased God.

John Baptizes Jesus

While Jesus was growing up in the town of Nazareth, His cousin, John, was growing up in Judea. John was now a man, thirty years old.

And John did not dress like the men in the city. He did not wear nice clothes. His clothes were made of camel's hair, and he wore a leather belt. He did not eat like most people eat either. He ate what he could find in the desert—locusts and wild honey. While John was in the desert, he learned what God wanted him to do.

One day John went to the Jordan River where he began preaching. "Stop doing wrong things," he told the people. "Obey God and get ready for His kingdom."

And many people believed what John said. To show that they were sorry they had not been doing what God wanted them to do, the people were baptized.

One day when John was preaching and baptizing in the river, Jesus came to him. "I want to be baptized," Jesus said to John.

Now John knew that Jesus had not done anything wrong. He knew that Jesus was God's Son. He was not like any of the other people.

"Oh! no," said John. "I should be asking You to baptize me."

But Jesus said, "I want to be baptized because God wants me to." So John baptized Jesus in the Jordan River.

Jesus prayed as John baptized Him. And as He came up out of the water, the skies were opened, and the Spirit of God came down from Heaven in the form of a beautiful dove. Suddenly, a voice from Heaven said, "This is my Son. I love Him, and am pleased with Him."

Jesus Chooses Helpers

Jesus had chosen twelve special helpers to be with Him all the time. They traveled with Jesus. They ate when He ate, listened when He talked, and tried very hard to follow Jesus in everything He did.

It had not been easy for Jesus to choose these twelve special workers. He had prayed all night long, before He began to choose them.

Jesus had gone up on a mountain to be alone with God. He wanted to pray to His Father in Heaven. He wanted to ask God to help Him choose His helpers.

As Jesus climbed up onto the mountain, He was thinking very hard. *Whom shall I choose to help me? I need twelve special men who will work very hard. They must be the best men I can find.*

Jesus prayed all night long! It was morning when He stopped praying. Jesus had asked God to help Him choose the best men for His special work. Now He was ready to begin selecting the twelve.

No one knows why Jesus decided to have just twelve special disciples. He could have had more. He could have had less. But Jesus chose just twelve.

After the night in prayer, Jesus began to form His special group. The first disciple He asked to help Him was Andrew, a fisherman. Andrew was so excited about helping Jesus, he couldn't wait to tell his brother. He said, "I have a brother named Simon Peter. I know he will want to be a special helper for Jesus, too."

Do you think Peter wanted to be a disciple of Jesus? Yes, he did! In fact Peter became one of the greatest preachers who ever lived.

These were the first two disciples. There were ten

more to be chosen. Jesus next asked two more brothers, James and John. They agreed right away to help Jesus. They didn't hesitate or worry about leaving their fishing boats. They wanted to help Jesus most of all.

Now Jesus had four helpers. But He kept choosing more. He asked two men named Philip and Bartholomew.

The seventh was a tax collector named Matthew. Many people were very surprised that Jesus would ask a tax collector to be one of His special helpers. But He did. Jesus knew Matthew would be a good worker.

Jesus continued to choose the twelve. He now had seven. Who would the other five be? The answer came soon. They were Thomas, another James who was the son of Alpheus, and another Simon who was called Zelotes. This made the number ten. Only two left to choose.

The last two men had the same name—Judas. But they were very different from each other. One was Judas the brother of James, and the other was Judas Iscariot.

Now Jesus had completed selecting the twelve. But why had He chosen them? What kind of work do you think Jesus wanted these men to do? He wanted them to be preachers! They were the ones who would preach to the whole world about Jesus. They would start the church when Jesus went back to Heaven.

Jesus taught His twelve special disciples exactly what He wanted them to preach. He lived with them and talked to them every day. He gave them special powers so they could heal sick people just by touching them. This healing power caused people to come to the twelve for help. Then they could tell those people about Jesus and His love for them.

A Crippled Man

Many people were crowded into a house in the city of Capernaum. They wanted to hear what Jesus would say. Some people came because they heard that Jesus had healed people of all kinds of sicknesses.

Four men came to the house carrying a sick friend on a mattress.

"Please let us in," they begged the men and women in the house. "We want Jesus to heal our friend. Please let us through."

But there were too many people. There was no way for them to get into the house.

"I have an idea," said one of the men. "There are steps leading up to the roof. Let's climb them."

Up, up climbed the friends very carefully with their friend. The man was paralyzed. He couldn't even wiggle his toes, much less walk. When the kind men got to the top of the stairs, they laid the mattress down on the flat roof.

Chip, chip, chip. The men worked at loosening the tiles on the roof. Soon there was a hole in the roof big enough for the mattress to go through.

Very carefully the friends fastened ropes around the mattress of the sick man. Even more carefully, they lowered their friend into the room where Jesus was.

Jesus looked at the man who could not move at all and said, "Get up, pick up your bed, and go home." And right away the man did just that. He got up, picked up his bed, and said, "Thank You, God," all the way home.

The people could hardly believe what had happened! They began praising God because Jesus had made the crippled man walk.

Jesus Feeds a Big Crowd

Jesus wanted to be alone. He was sad because His cousin, John, had been killed by wicked King Herod. So Jesus and His disciples got into a boat to sail across the Sea of Galilee.

While Jesus and His disciples were crossing to the other side of the sea, many people were bringing sick friends and relatives for Jesus to heal. They were waiting by the Sea of Galilee for Jesus to come. After waiting awhile, the people began to worry.

"Where is Jesus?" they asked each other. "We have come a long way to see Him."

Someone said, "I saw Jesus and His disciples go across the sea in a boat. It may be a long time before He comes back here."

The people didn't want to wait a long time to see Jesus. They said, "Let's save time. Let's walk around the lake to where Jesus is. Then we can see Him today, and ask Him to help us."

When Jesus' boat landed on the other side of the sea, He saw a big crowd of people waiting—the old, the young, the crippled, the blind, the very, very sick, and He loved them all. Jesus wanted to help every one of them and He did. He healed all the sick people. Then He taught everyone there about the love of God.

It must have taken a long time to heal the men and women, boys and girls who wanted Jesus' help. It had been a long day. It would be night soon because the sun was going down.

Jesus looked at the big crowd of people. Then He said to His disciple, Philip, "The people are hungry. Where can we buy bread to feed all of them?"

Philip said, "Master, we don't have enough money to buy bread and give everyone even a small piece."

Jesus knew that, and He knew how He was going to feed the people.

Jesus said, "Go and see how many loaves of bread you can find in the crowd."

And His disciple, Andrew, said, "A young boy has five barley loaves and two fish that he will share. But how can that feed so many people?"

Jesus had a plan, and He was also able to do wonderful things. "Tell the people to sit down in groups on the green grass," Jesus told His disciples. And the people sat down in groups, with fifty in some groups and one hundred in others. The disciples counted more than five thousand men. There were also women and children there who weren't counted.

Jesus took the five barley loaves the little boy gave, looked up toward Heaven and thanked God for them. Jesus also took the two fish, and again looked up toward Heaven and thanked God for them.

Then Jesus began breaking the five small loaves of barley bread and the two fish into pieces and putting them in baskets. Then His disciples passed the baskets of bread and fish among the people seated on the soft, green grass. And everyone, every man, woman, boy, and girl ate until they were full.

When everyone was through eating, Jesus told His disciples, "Gather the food that the people didn't eat so that nothing will be wasted."

And when they had gathered up the bread and fish left over, the disciples counted twelve baskets full. The little boy's lunch had been enough to feed all of the people. Jesus had made it more than enough.

The Lost Son

Jesus told a story one day about a father and his two sons. The older son worked hard and did everything his father told him to do. But the younger son was not happy. He wanted to leave home.

"Give me my part of the money now, Dad," he said. "I want to leave home. I'll travel to faraway places, find new friends, and have a lot of fun."

The father was very sad to see his young son leave home. But he gave him the money and watched him go.

The young man traveled to a faraway country. He did find a lot of new friends. They saw how much money he had to spend. They helped him spend it, too.

Then one day the young man looked in his money bag. Do you know what he found? Nothing! It was empty! He had spent all the money his father had given him!

Soon he was hungry. He had no place to sleep. His clothes became old rags. He had no friends now. No one would give him food or help him. Finally, the young man got a job feeding pigs.

"Oh, I wish I'd never left home!" he said.

He thought about home. He missed his father. He missed his brother, too.

"Even my father's servants have more food to eat than they need. If I were one of my own father's servants, I'd at least have food to eat. I know what I'll do. I'll go home! I'll ask my father if I can work for him."

Right then the young man started home. It was a long way back home.

Finally, he could see his home in the distance. He could see a man standing near the house. Was that his father? Yes, it was!

The father had been standing, looking down the road. He, too, saw his son in the distance.

"Is that my son who left home?" asked the father. Yes! It was! The father began to run to meet his son. He couldn't run fast enough. When he reached his son, he hugged him! He kissed him. He hugged him again!

"Father, I did wrong in leaving home," said the son. "I'm sorry now. I am no longer good enough to be your son. Will you just let me work for you as one of your servants?"

"No, no! my son," said the father. "I am so happy to have you back home! You are my son who was lost. You are now found.

"Servants," said the father, "bring some clothes for my son. Put a ring on his finger. Put shoes on his feet. Cook a big dinner for him to eat. Let's all be happy. My son is back home!"

Jesus told this story to show us how much God loves us. He said the father is like God. And the boy who left home is like each one of us when we go away from God and do things we know are wrong. But God always forgives us and welcomes us back, just like the father in the story.

Jesus Finds a
Friend in a Tree

Jesus and His disciples were walking toward the city of Jericho. This was the city where Joshua and his army had once marched around the city walls, and God had made the walls fall down.

As Jesus and His twelve helpers entered Jericho, a crowd was already waiting along the streets. One of the men waiting to see Jesus was a tax collector named Zaccheus. Zaccheus had heard about the wonderful things Jesus did—like making a blind man see—and Zaccheus wanted to see Jesus. But Zaccheus was not very tall, and he couldn't get through the crowd.

"Excuse me, sir. Pardon me," Zaccheus may have said. But as Jesus came closer and closer to Zaccheus, the people crowded closer and closer to each other and to the path where Jesus was walking.

Zaccheus wanted to see Jesus. But how could he? He looked around and quickly came up with an answer to his problem.

"I know what I'll do," he said to himself. *"I will run farther down the road and climb into a tree so I will be above the people. Then no one will be in my way, and I can see Jesus."*

And that's exactly what Zaccheus did. He grabbed a limb and pulled himself up and climbed until he was high enough to see Jesus.

"Here He comes," people were saying. "Jesus is coming this way."

Zaccheus was all ready. He shaded his eyes with his hand so he could see Jesus better. Jesus and His friends

91

walked closer and closer. Zaccheus could feel his heart beating faster and faster. Suddenly, the little man got a big surprise. Jesus stopped right under the tree where Zaccheus was sitting.

Zaccheus wondered what was going to happen next, but he didn't have to wait long. Jesus looked right up at him and said, "Zaccheus, hurry and come down. Today I must stay at your house."

And that's exactly what happened. Zaccheus hurried down from the tree and took Jesus to his house. Zaccheus was very, very happy.

Now, a lot of people in Jericho did not like Zaccheus because he collected tax money for the Roman government, and because he was rich. Most of the tax collectors were very rich because they cheated people. The people knew the tax collectors often took more money for taxes than the people really owed. Then they kept the extra money for themselves.

Or maybe they were jealous because Jesus was going to Zaccheus' house. So when they saw Jesus going with Zaccheus, they grumbled and said, "Jesus is going to stay at the house of a bad man. We don't think Jesus should do that."

Zaccheus did not worry about what people were saying. At his house, he stood and said, "I will give half of what I have to the poor, and if I have taken too much tax money from anyone, I will give back four times as much to that person." Zaccheus wanted to do what was right. He was very happy and very thankful.

"Today, Zaccheus," Jesus said, "you have learned what it means to be saved. You have learned how to live. I came to earth to help people like you. I came to find people who need my help and show them how to live."

Jesus and the Children

Jesus talked about God in such a loving way that mothers wanted Him to hold their children and ask God to bless them. One day after Jesus had been teaching, the women started bringing their babies and other young children to see Jesus.

Some women carried babies in their arms, and some children walked beside them. This was exciting to the mothers and children.

"There He is!" they said. "I see Jesus."

The children were smiling and laughing. Jesus was smiling because He loved them so. But Jesus' helpers were not smiling.

They may have thought that Jesus was too tired to welcome the babies and children. They said to the mothers, "Stop! Go away. Jesus does not have time for children. He has more important work to do. Leave Him alone."

The mothers and children stopped. They were so disappointed. They couldn't talk to Jesus.

But before they could say anything, the mothers and the children heard a kind voice saying, "Let the children come to me. Don't stop them." It was Jesus.

Then He said, "God's kingdom is for people like these children. They love me and are happy to do what I ask."

Jesus loved the children. He picked them up and held them in His arms.

He touched each child and prayed to God. Perhaps He said, "Father, bless these children. Keep them healthy. Help them to be good and obey You. May they love You as You love them." The Bible says that Jesus blessed the children again and again that day.

Children Praise Jesus

Jesus was a king. But He was not the kind of king who sits on a throne and rules a country. Jesus was the King of everyone who would love and obey God.

The Jewish people had waited a long time for the kind of king Jesus was. They had waited a long time for the Savior, God would send.

God had promised Abraham, Isaac, and Jacob that He would bless everyone through Someone born into their family. Hundreds of years later, that special person was born. He was Jesus, God's own Son.

Jesus knew that it was time to let the people know that He was the King God had promised to send. He told two of His disciples, "Go to the town near you, and there you will find a mother donkey and her baby colt. Tell whoever speaks to you that the Lord needs them, and right away that person will send the donkeys with you."

Jesus knew that the Bible said, "Your king is coming to you, riding on a donkey."

The disciples went to the town and got the donkeys just as Jesus told them. They spread their coats on the young donkey so Jesus could ride on it. Then Jesus began His slow, bumpy ride up the hill to Jerusalem.

It was Passover time again—time for the people to worship at the temple. The city was crowded, and many people were so sure that Jesus was going to be their king, that they greeted Him in a special way. They cut palm branches from the trees and spread them in the road for Jesus' donkey to walk on. Many people put their outer coats in the road, too, so the donkey carrying Jesus could walk on them.

When the people saw Jesus coming into the city of Jerusalem riding on the donkey, they waved palm branches and praised Him saying, "Hosanna to the Son of David. Blessed is He who comes in the name of the Lord. Hosanna in the highest."

What a sight! Jesus riding on the donkey and hundreds of people on the streets and in the windows, waving branches and shouting.

In Jerusalem Jesus got off the donkey and walked into the temple where He healed people who could not see or walk. And even in the temple, children were shouting to Jesus, "Hosanna to the Son of David!"

Some of the teachers in the temple did not want Jesus to be their king, and they did not believe God had sent Him. It made them angry to hear the children praising Jesus. They said to Him, "Do you hear what the children are saying?"

"Yes," Jesus said, "God is letting these children praise me with these words. He is happy with them." And Jesus was pleased with the children, too, because He loved them very much.

A Special Supper

Jesus and His twelve disciples were all together for the last time. And everything was ready for them to eat the Passover meal together.

Jesus knew that He would not be with His disciples much longer. So that evening, Jesus took a towel and tied it around His waist. Then he poured water into a bowl, kneeled down on the floor, and washed His disciples' feet. Then He dried them with the towel. Jesus went around the table and washed and dried the feet of each of His disciples.

When He finished, He sat back down at His place at the table. Then Jesus said, "I am your Teacher and Lord, and I have washed your feet. If I am willing to be a servant to you, then you should be willing to be a servant to others."

And while they were eating, Jesus did something else for the disciples to remember. He took a piece of bread, thanked God for it, and broke it into pieces. Then He gave the pieces to His friends and said, "This bread is like my body which will be nailed to the cross and broken for you. Eat the bread to remember me."

Then Jesus took a cup of grape juice and thanked God for it. He passed it around for His disciples to drink.

"This juice is like my blood that I will shed on the cross," Jesus said. "Drink the juice to remember me."

Peter and Andrew, James and John, and the other disciples did not understand that Jesus would die soon. But after He died, arose, and went back to Heaven, they ate the bread and drank the grape juice just as Jesus told them. They remembered everything Jesus had said and what He had done for them.

The Saddest Day

Jesus' friends were sad. They could hardly believe what was happening. Jesus was sad, too. He knew that some bad men wanted to kill Him. They were looking everywhere for Jesus. Soon they would find Him.

So after their time together at the Passover supper, Jesus and His disciples went to a garden to pray. Jesus wanted to pray in a quiet place because He was so sad. Jesus knew where a nice quiet place was—a garden where olive trees grew. Jesus had been in this garden before. The garden was called Gethsemane.

While Jesus was praying in the garden, Judas Iscariot came with the bad men. He pointed to Jesus and some soldiers arrested Him like He was a criminal. They grabbed Jesus and took Him away.

Jesus had not done anything wrong, but some people did not like Him. They did not believe He was God's Son. So they told lies about Jesus. Then they got the Roman governor, Pilate, to say Jesus must be crucified. He must be nailed to a cross like a criminal to die.

The Roman soldiers beat Jesus. They made fun of Him because He said He was a king. They put a crown of thorns on His head and a purple robe around His shoulders. They spit on Him and slapped Him.

Jesus walked down the street, carrying a wooden cross on His back. He was so weak and the cross was so heavy that He fell down. Then the soldiers made a man named Simon carry Jesus' cross the rest of the way.

A lot of people followed Jesus. Some of them cried. They knew what the soldiers were going to do. At the top of a hill, Jesus was nailed to a cross. Two other men, both of them bad men, were nailed to crosses too.

One was on a cross to the right of Jesus, and the other on a cross to the left of Him. Above Jesus' head on the cross was a sign that read *King of the Jews.*

Jesus' disciples, His mother, and other friends stood watching. They were very sad to see Jesus hanging there. They did not want to leave Him alone. Jesus had done nothing wrong, but He looked at the soldiers and said, "Father, forgive them because they do not know what they are doing." Jesus was not angry.

One of the men on a cross beside Jesus said, "Jesus, remember me when You come into Your kingdom."

Jesus said, "Today you will be with me in Paradise."

Jesus was not afraid to die. He knew what God was going to do. He knew that after He died, no one who believed in God would need to be afraid to die. But His friends did not understand this yet. They felt very sad.

While Jesus was on the cross, He did something else for someone. He had already asked God to forgive the soldiers who crucified Him. He had already forgiven the robber and promised that He would be with Him when he died. Now Jesus did something special for His mother, Mary. He looked at her and His disciple, John, who were standing near the cross with some women.

Then Jesus said, "Woman, look at your son." But Jesus did not mean himself. Then He said to John, "Look at your mother." They knew what Jesus meant. From that time on, John took care of Mary as a member of his own family.

When Jesus had done everything God wanted Him to, He said, "It is finished." Then He died.

Later, two men, Joseph of Arimathea and Nicodemus, took Jesus' body, wrapped it in nice linen cloth with sweet-smelling spices and laid it in a new grave in a garden.

The Happiest Day

After Jesus died, His friends buried His body. Then Pilate had the grave opening covered with a big stone, and put Roman soldiers by the grave to guard it. Pilate was afraid that someone would steal Jesus' body and then say that He had risen from the dead. Pilate thought Jesus had caused a lot of trouble, and he didn't want any more trouble.

Peter and Andrew, James and John, and the other disciples were so sad because Jesus had been crucified. And the women who followed Jesus were sad too. Everyone who loved Him knew He had done nothing wrong. He didn't deserve to die. Jesus had loved and helped everyone.

Sunday morning came, and Mary Magdalene went to the garden where Jesus was buried. She was bringing sweet-smelling spices to put by His body. But when she got to the grave, she was surprised. The big stone had been rolled away from the door to the grave.

"Oh, no!" Mary thought. *"Jesus' body has been moved. Where could it be?"* Then she hurried away to tell Simon Peter and John.

While Mary was gone, several other women came to the grave and found it empty. They didn't know what could have happened to Jesus' body either.

Then suddenly, the women saw two men standing beside them in shining white clothes. They were so afraid that they couldn't look at the men.

One of the angels said, "Why are you looking for Jesus here among the dead people? He is not here. He has risen. Remember what He told you? He said that bad men would crucify Him, but on the third day He would rise

Jesus' Special Friends Do His Special Work

H. Petach

again." Now the women remembered. They hurried to tell the disciples what the angels said.

Mary Magdalene came to Simon Peter and John before the other women and said, "They have taken Jesus out of the grave, and we don't know where they have put Him."

Peter and John were surprised, too. They ran as fast as they could to the garden where Jesus had been buried. John got to the grave first, but he didn't go in. When Peter arrived, he went in and saw the cloths that had been wrapped around Jesus. But there was no body.

Then John went inside the tomb, too, and saw that it was empty. Then they both knew what Mary Magdalene had said was true.

Mary Magdalene was so sad. She stood outside the empty grave crying. While she was crying, she bent down and looked into the tomb. She was surprised to see two angels dressed in white. One angel was sitting where Jesus' head had been; the other angel where His feet had been. The angels asked Mary, "Woman, why are you crying?"

"Because they have taken Jesus away, and I don't know where they have put Him," she said, still crying.

Then Mary turned around. A man was standing there.

The man asked, "Woman, why are you crying? Who are you looking for?"

Mary thought He might be the gardener, so she said, "Sir, if you have taken Jesus away, tell me where He is."

The man spoke again. "Mary!" He said. Now Mary knew who He was.

She turned to Him and said, "Teacher!"

Mary wasn't sad any more. She had seen Jesus. He was alive!

Jesus Returns to Heaven and His Church Begins

Jesus knew it was time for Him to leave the earth. He had not planned to stay with His friends very long. He had come to work, and now His work was all done. It was time for Him to go back to His Father in Heaven. It was also time for Jesus' disciples to do their special work.

Jesus told Peter and the other disciples, "After I leave you, I will ask God to send the Holy Spirit to help you. But you must wait in Jerusalem until God sends you this power from Heaven."

Jesus took His friends to the top of a mountain. They knew something was about to happen. They watched Jesus closely. Then He raised His hands and asked God to bless them. And as the eleven disciples watched, Jesus began to go up into the air, right off the ground! He was going up and up, higher and higher. Nothing was picking Him up. His body was just rising up and up. Jesus was going back to Heaven.

The disciples watched until they could not see Him anymore. And while they were staring into the sky, two men in white appeared and said, "Why are you men standing here looking into the sky? Jesus has gone back to Heaven. Someday He will come back from Heaven in the same way."

The eleven disciples went back to Jerusalem and chose a twelfth disciple to take Judas Iscariot's place. Then they waited for God's power to come as Jesus had promised.

On a special day called Pentecost, many of Jesus'

friends were together in Jerusalem. Peter and the other disciples were there too. Suddenly, three surprising things happened. A very loud noise that sounded like a strong wind filled the house where they were. Then a small flame of fire was in the air over each disciple's head, and each of them began speaking in other languages. God's Holy Spirit had given them the power that Jesus promised before He went back to Heaven.

Many men and women from different countries were staying in Jerusalem. They had come for a special worship time to remember God's law. They heard the loud noise, too, and came to where the apostles were. The people were very surprised.

"How can we hear what they are saying in our own languages?" they asked. "These men are not from our countries. They are from Galilee. What does this mean?"

Then Peter stood up and told everyone what the loud noise and the flames and the speaking in other languages meant. Peter said, "God has sent this power just as He sent Jesus. Although bad men nailed Jesus to a cross, God made Him alive again. Jesus is at the right hand of God now. He is the Lord and King that the Bible said was coming. And if you are sorry for the things you have done wrong, God will forgive you. Then He will give you the power of the Holy Spirit to help you. God has made this promise to you and to your children and to everyone who loves and obeys Him."

When the people heard what Peter said, they wanted to obey God. They wanted to have their sins forgiven. That day, three thousand people were baptized.

This was the kingdom Jesus had talked about. He was king in Heaven. The people who obeyed Him and were baptized were called His church.

A Prayer Meeting

John Mark, his mother, and their Christian friends were having a prayer meeting. They were asking God to protect Peter and keep him safe, because a wicked king had put Peter in jail.

Was Peter afraid? Was he worried? No, not at all. He was sound asleep between two guards in his prison cell.

While Peter was sleeping and his friends were praying, God was doing His work. Suddenly, an angel appeared and a light shone into Peter's dark cell. The angel touched Peter's side, woke him up, and said, "Get up, quickly."

The guards did not move. They did not see the angel or the light. They did not see the chains fall off Peter's hands, or hear the angel say, "Put on your clothes and your sandals. Wrap your coat around you, and follow me." God had closed the eyes of the guards so none of them saw Peter follow the angel out of the prison.

Peter did what the angel asked. Peter kept following the angel. He followed the angel outside of the prison and into a street. Then suddenly the angel was gone.

Peter hurried to the house of John Mark and his mother, Mary. He knocked on their door.

Rhoda, the servant girl, heard Peter. But she was so excited, she didn't open the door. She ran to tell the others the good news and left Peter standing outside.

Rhoda ran right into the prayer meeting and said, "Peter is standing at the door!"

The Christians were happy to hear how God had sent His angel to save Peter. They said, "Thank You, God, for hearing our prayers. Thank You for taking care of our friend, Peter."

Saul Becomes a Friend

Saul was angry. *"Who do those Christians think they are?"* he thought to himself. *"They really believe that Jesus was the Son of God. And that preacher, Stephen, had the nerve to call the Jewish leaders killers and betrayers! He deserved to die. He was an enemy of God."*

Saul was a young man who knew a lot about the Bible, but he did not understand that Jesus was the Savior the Bible talked about.

"I want the names of all Christians," Saul said. "I want to arrest them and put them into prison."

Then a preacher named Stephen was stoned to death for teaching about Jesus. Saul held the coats of the men, while they threw big rocks at Stephen and killed him. Saul believed he was doing the right thing. He thought that Stephen was bad and deserved to die.

Saul was so angry with the Christians that he went to the high priest of the temple in Jerusalem and asked permission to look for Christians in the city of Damascus. He wanted to arrest them and bring them back to Jerusalem. Saul really believed that the Christians were enemies of God, but Saul himself was the real enemy of God.

Saul started on his trip to Damascus with some of his friends. Suddenly, a bright light from the sky flashed around him, and Saul fell to the ground. Then, he heard a voice, saying, "Saul, Saul, why are you hurting me?"

"Who are you, Lord?" Saul asked. And the voice said, "I am Jesus, and you are hurting me. Get up and go into the city, and you will be told what you must do."

Saul got up from the ground and opened his eyes. He couldn't see anything! Saul was blind. His friends had to

take him by the hand and lead him into the city of Damascus.

Saul had a lot to think about while he was blind. Before he lost his sight, he had seen and heard Jesus. Saul may have thought about Stephen, too, and all of the other Christians he had arrested. Now he knew that Jesus was alive.

God had plans for Saul to work for Him. So He spoke in a vision to a Christian named Ananias, who lived in the city of Damascus.

"Ananias," Jesus called.

"What do You want, Lord?" Ananias answered.

Jesus told Ananias, "Get up and go to the house of a man named Judas on Straight Street. Ask to see a man named Saul because Saul has been praying. This man Saul has seen a vision of a man coming to touch him and make him see again. Ananias, you are that man."

Ananias said, "Lord, I have heard that Saul did a lot to hurt the Christians in Jerusalem. He has come here to Damascus with permission to arrest everyone who prays in Your name."

Jesus said, "Do what I tell you because I have chosen Saul to teach about me. He will preach in my name to Jews, to people who are not Jews, and even to kings. And he will have to suffer because he believes in me."

Ananias obeyed Jesus. He went to the house of Judas and put his hands on Saul's head. Ananias said, "Brother Saul, Jesus has sent me to you so that you can see again and have the help of the Holy Spirit."

And right away, flakes of skin fell from Saul's eyes, and he could see. Then Saul got up and let Ananias baptize him. Saul was now a Christian. He began to teach in the synagogues in Damascus. Saul told the people, "Jesus is the Son of God."

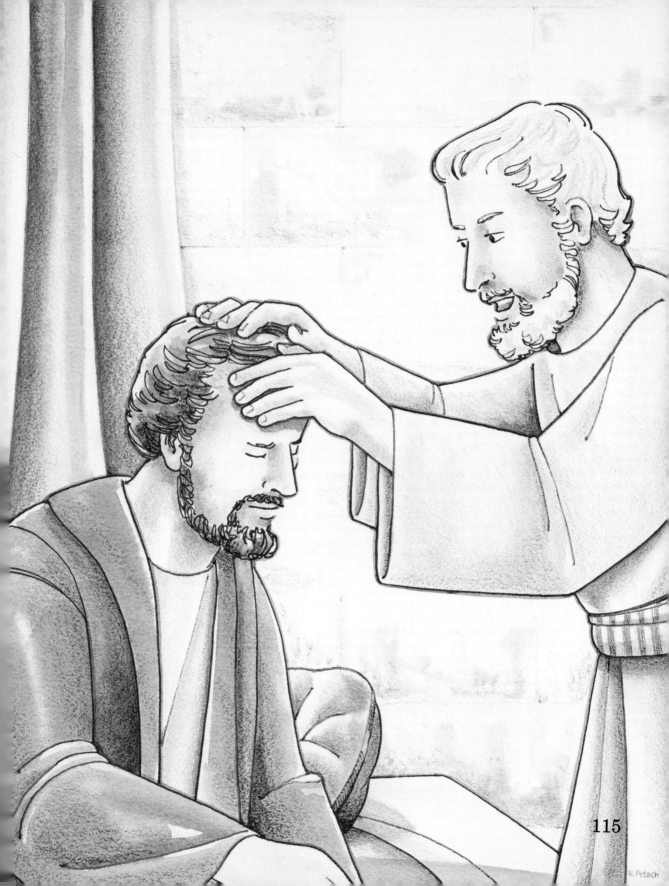

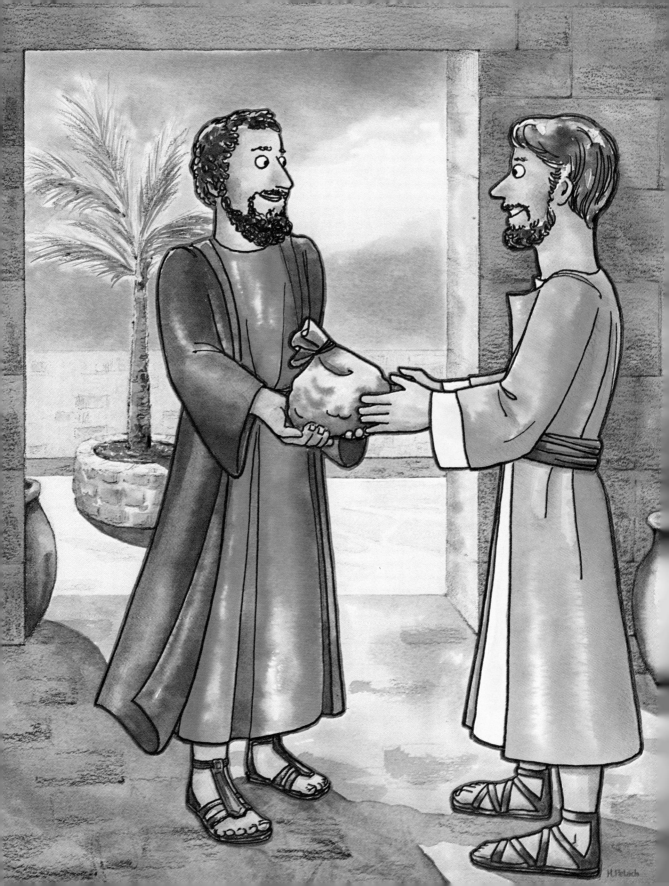

Barnabas, a Kind Helper

Wonderful things happened when Jesus' helpers started His church. Many people believed in Jesus and were baptized. Then the new Christians stayed in Jerusalem to learn all they could from Peter and John and the other men who had been with Jesus. Some of them did not have enough money to stay for a long time in the city, so the Christians who lived in Jerusalem said, "We will take care of you. You may stay with us."

These first Christians shared what they had. Some of them came to Peter and the other apostles with money and said, "We sold our houses and our land. Take this money and share it with the people who need help." One of the men who sold a field he owned and brought the money to the church leaders was Barnabas.

Barnabas was a good man. He had always obeyed the laws of God. And when he learned that Jesus was the Savior promised by God, Barnabas was baptized and became a Christian.

Then Barnabas went to Antioch where he found many new Christians. This made Barnabas happy.

There were more and more Christians all of the time, which made a lot of work for Barnabas. He needed help and so he went to the city of Tarsus to find Saul. Saul agreed to help Barnabas and they worked together in Antioch for a year, helping the new followers of Jesus.

The Christians in Antioch were like the Christians in Jerusalem. They were helpful and loved each other. When they heard that there was not enough food in Judea, and the Christians there were hungry, they gave money to help them. They sent the money to the leaders of the church in Jerusalem by Barnabas and Saul.

A Young Helper

Saul and Barnabas began traveling to many cities and countries, teaching about Jesus. Then Saul's name was changed to Paul. From then on he was called Paul.

One of the cities Paul visited was Lystra. There he met a young man named Timothy. Timothy had been taught the stories in the Bible from the time he was a very young boy. His mother, Eunice, and his grandmother, Lois, taught him about God. And when Paul came to Lystra, Timothy learned about Jesus.

Later, when Paul came back to Lystra, he was looking for a helper. He wanted someone to travel with him and help him tell people about Jesus. Paul said to Timothy, "I want you to come with me, Timothy. The Christians here at Lystra and those in Iconium have told me how much you love Jesus. You are the kind of person I am looking for. You can help Jesus' church to grow." So Timothy traveled with Paul to many different cities, teaching and helping in whatever way he could.

Later, when Paul was put in prison for teaching about Jesus, Timothy kept on working for Jesus. And Paul wrote letters to Timothy to help him.

In his letters to Timothy, Paul said, "Pray for everyone, because God wants everyone to be in His church. Teach the people what I have taught you. Be a good example to the other Christians by what you say and by the way you live. Love others and always believe in God and Jesus. Keep teaching and studying, and you will save yourself and the people who listen to you."

Timothy remembered what his mother and grandmother and Paul had taught him. He grew up to be a good helper for Jesus.

A Terrible Shipwreck

Paul was arrested and put in jail several times. He finally decided that he wanted the emperor who lived in Rome to decide whether he had done anything wrong. So Paul was put on a ship going to Italy so he could see Caesar, the emperor, in Rome.

There were many people on the ship with Paul—a Roman centurion, soldiers, sailors, other prisoners, and Paul's friends, Luke and Aristarchus.

The ship was carrying grain. And it was the fall of the year when the seas were rough, so the ship had to go very slowly. Paul told the captain and the other men running the ship, "This trip will end in trouble. The weather is bad this time of year. The grain, the ship, and our own lives could be lost."

The captain of the ship didn't believe Paul. And the Roman officer guarding him believed the captain and the ship's owner instead of Paul.

Paul's friend, Luke, wrote about what happened in the book of Acts in the Bible.

"A strong wind like a hurricane blew on our ship and pushed us. The sailors tied heavy ropes around the boat to keep the wind from tearing it apart. We were afraid of being driven onto quicksand.

"We worked hard fighting the storm," Luke said. "And on the second day, the sailors had to throw the grain overboard to make the boat lighter so it wouldn't sink. On the third day, they threw the ship's extra equipment into the sea. And for several days, the storm was so bad that we couldn't see the sun or the stars. There was no way to tell what direction we were going. And we hadn't eaten for several days. No one believed that we would live, except Paul.

"Then Paul stood among this frightened group of people and said, 'Men, if you had listened to me and stayed in port when I told you, we would not have had these problems and lost our grain and gear from the ship. But be happy because no one will lose his life. Only the ship will be lost. I know this is true because an angel of God came to me tonight and said, 'Don't be afraid, Paul. You will make it to Rome to see the emperor, and God will save the lives of everyone on the ship with you.' And I believe that God will do what He said. We will be saved, but our ship will wreck on an island.' "

Luke continued his story. "After being tossed around the seas for two weeks, the sailors thought we were coming closer to land. They put four anchors down into the water to slow the ship and keep it from wrecking. Then the sailors tried to escape in a small boat, but Paul said, 'If these men don't stay on the ship, the rest of you can't be saved.'

"So the soldiers cut the ropes holding the small boat and let it fall into the sea. And when it was nearly daylight, the sailors saw land. They tried to guide the ship to a beach, but it ran aground. The front of it stuck and wouldn't move, and the waves broke the back of the ship.

"Then the soldiers wanted to kill the prisoners so they couldn't swim away and escape. But the centurion wanted to keep Paul alive so he wouldn't let anyone be killed. The centurion said, 'Everyone who can swim, go ahead and swim to land. The rest of you float on planks of wood or whatever you can find from the ship.' And that is exactly what they did. Just as God had promised Paul, all two hundred and seventy-six people made it safely to land."

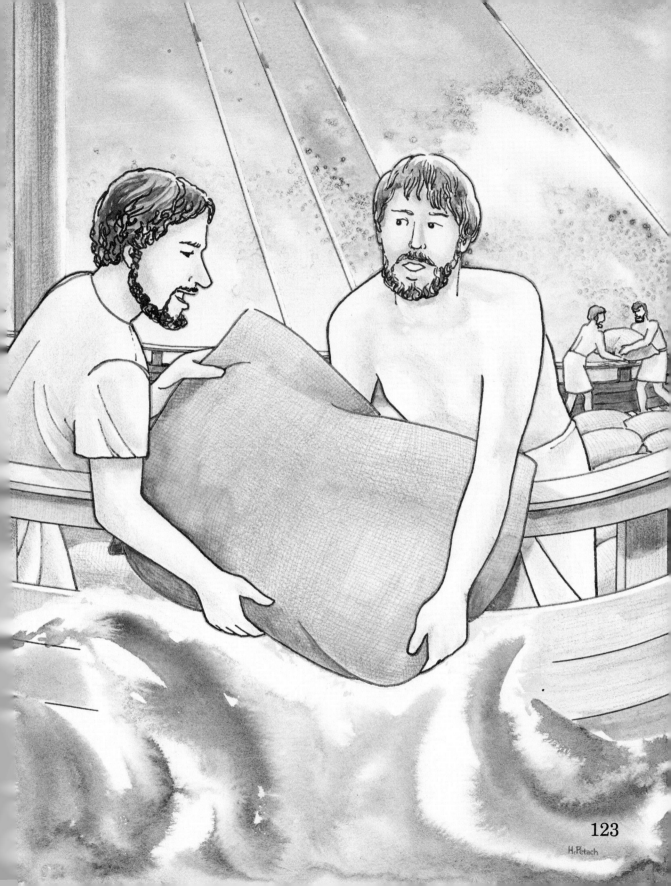

123

Heaven: Our Special Home

John Sees the Heavenly City

The Bible tells us about God and His Son, Jesus. It tells us why God put people on the earth.

A long time ago God had Moses write about the beginning of the world. Then later God had His servant, John, write about Heaven, because Heaven is the new world where the people who love and obey God will live someday.

John was an old man when he wrote about Heaven. He was a prisoner on an island called Patmos. John and many other followers of Jesus were arrested and punished for being Christians and teaching about Him. But John was glad he had done what he could for Jesus.

One special day God showed John in a vision what Heaven would look like. John may have thought he was dreaming, but he knew that what he saw was true. And John wrote about what he saw that day because God told him to.

John wrote, "I saw a new Heaven and a new earth. The old Heaven and the old earth were gone. And I saw the holy city, the new Jerusalem, coming down out of Heaven from God. It was as beautiful as a bride coming to meet her husband.

"And I heard a loud voice say, 'God will be with His people and live with them. And they will not be sad anymore. God will wipe the tears from their eyes. No one will die anymore. No one will cry. No one will hurt.'"

And from the throne of Heaven, John heard the words, "I will make everything new."

In his vision, John was carried away to a high mountain where he could see the holy city. It shone as bright as crystal because God was there.

Heaven was like a great big square city, but it was more beautiful than any city on earth. The outside wall of the city was made of jasper. It shone bright and clear. The inside of the city was made of gold, and it was built on precious stones—red, green, blue, and every color of the rainbow. The twelve gates of the city were made of pearls, and the streets were pure gold. It was the most beautiful city anyone could imagine.

John said, "There was no temple in the new Jerusalem because God and Jesus themselves were there. The city did not need the sun or moon because God gave the people light. And nothing bad can ever go into the city.

"And I saw a river coming from the throne of God and Jesus. And on each side of the river were trees that grew fruit each month. They were called the tree of life."

John said, "I heard and saw these things I wrote about."

John wrote about the beautiful home that Jesus told Him to write about. Perhaps as he was writing, he remembered the words of Jesus before He was crucified. Jesus had said to His disciples, "Don't be worried or sad. You believe in God, and you believe in me. In Heaven where my Father is, there are many rooms. I am going back to Heaven to make a place for you so that someday you can come to Heaven and be with me. And one day I will come back for you."

Jesus told John, "Happy are the people who love and obey God. They will enter the heavenly city. They will live there forever."